T0388505

Access your online resources

Blob Bullying is accompanied by a number of printable online materials, designed to ensure this resource best supports your professional needs.

Activate your online resources:

Go to www.routledge.com/cw/speechmark and click on the cover of this book.

Click the 'Sign in or Request Access' button and follow the instructions in order to access the resources.

THE BLOB GUIDE TO

BLOB BULLYING

This practical and accessible resource contains a wealth of discussion sheets and games to help victims of bullying reflect and talk about their experiences and feelings using the internationally familiar Blob figures.

Diverse and inclusive, the Blob figures are a proven way to help children and adults share their feelings and experiences. Without age, culture or gender, they enable the individual to focus on feelings and body language. In this book, the Blobs explore bullying. From Blob Trees to Bingo games, cards and emotional scales, the Blobs provide a visual structure that allows children, teenagers and adults to open up about being bullied.

Offering unique activities that help scaffold conversations for people of all ages and abilities, this is an essential resource for teachers, teaching assistants, youth and social workers, psychologists, counsellors and all those who work with and have caring responsibilities for others.

Pip Wilson is the author of over 50 books and the famous Blob Tree tools, which can open the hardest heart, and is able to open up meaningful communication in all cultures and contexts.

Ian Long is an illustrator who has worked with Pip all of his adult life, drawing, creating and visualising ideas that they have imagined together since the early 1980s. He has been a youth and pastoral worker in Gloucestershire, a primary school teacher in West Sussex and Hampshire, a carer for his father who suffered with Alzheimer's and is now working full time on books.

Blobs

Blobs are delightful characters (without gender or age) that help facilitate and stimulate meaningful discussions about difficult issues or situations. Individuals or groups can start discussions by identifying themselves, or others, with an individual or group of Blobs whose actions or feelings represent their own.

The series includes a range of activities, books and posters, suitable for all ages.

Authors: Pip Wilson and Ian Long

Titles in this series include:

Blob Bullying

The Blob Guide to Children's Human Rights

The Big Book of Blobs (2nd edition)

The Big Book of Blob Trees (2nd edition)

The Big Book of Blob Feelings

The Big Book of Blob Feelings 2

The Blob Anger Book

Feelings Blob Cards

Emotions Blob Cards

Anger Blob Cards

Bereavement Blob Cards

Behaviour Blob Cards

Family Blob Cards

Teenage Life Blob Cards

Blob School

The Blob Visual Emotional Thesaurus

Giant Blob Tree Poster

Blob Feelings Ball

Blob Bullying

Pip Wilson + Ian Long

THE BLOB GUIDE TO

BLOB BULLYING

Pip Wilson and Ian Long

Routledge
Taylor & Francis Group

LONDON AND NEW YORK

THE BLOB GUIDE TO
BLOB BULLYING

Cover image: © Ian Long

First published 2023
by Routledge
4 Park Square, Milton Park, Abingdon, Oxon OX14 4RN

and by Routledge
605 Third Avenue, New York, NY 10158

Routledge is an imprint of the Taylor & Francis Group, an informa business

British Library Cataloguing-in-Publication Data
A catalogue record for this book is available from the British Library

Library of Congress Cataloging-in-Publication Data
Names: Wilson, Pip, author. | Long, Ian (Illustrator) author.
Title: Blob bullying / Pip Wilson and Ian Long.
Description: First Edition. | New York : Routledge, 2023. |
Series: Blobs Identifiers: LCCN 2022022375 | ISBN 9781032330488 (Hardback) |
ISBN 9781032330495 (Paperback) | ISBN 9781003317913 (eBook)
Subjects: LCSH: Bullying.
Classification: LCC BF637.B85 W55 2023 | DDC 302.34/3–dc23/eng/20220714
LC record available at https://lccn.loc.gov/2022022375

ISBN: 978-1-032-33048-8 (hbk)
ISBN: 978-1-032-33049-5 (pbk)
ISBN: 978-1-003-31791-3 (ebk)

DOI: 10.4324/9781003317913

Typeset in Helvetica
by Newgen Publishing UK

Access the companion website: www.routledge.com/cw/speechmark

Dedicated to all victims of bullying by individuals, groups and those in authority

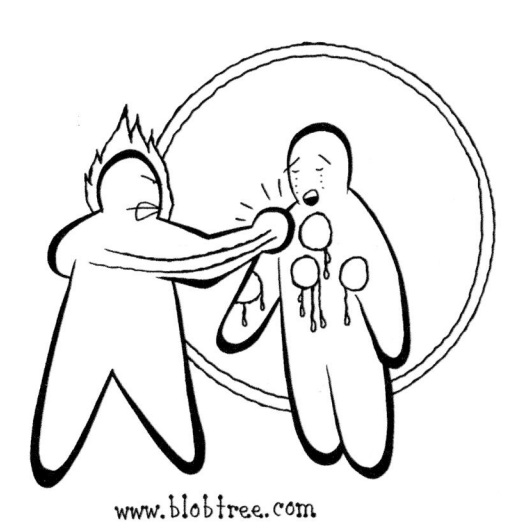

www.blobtree.com

Contents

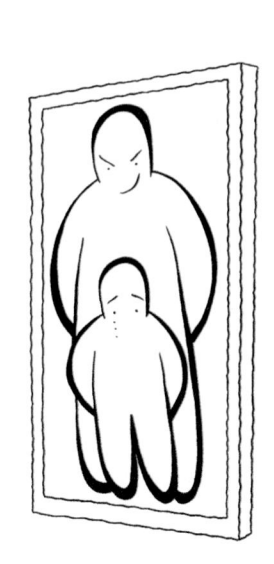

THE BLOB GUIDE TO
BLOB BULLYING

Introduction

Until we experience bullying as an adult, it can be something we imagine to be restricted to a childhood playground encounter. In this introduction, Ian Long recounts his experiences of bullying.

I can recall the many times I was verbally bullied by my classmates in my secondary school, and the times I verbally bullied others. We probably all have some memories of when we were picked on during our formative years. People can be picked on for their names, height, weight, appearance, wealth, freckles, friends, abilities, in fact almost anything. What is less clearly understood is the way in which adults actively engage in this behaviour. Let me relate just one such personal anecdote.

My first job as a teacher was very exciting. I clearly remember my first class, my first day and the feeling of pleasure of marking my first set of books. I was a primary school teacher for seventeen years. It was a job I enjoyed and did pretty well in, but that didn't prevent me from being bullied throughout the whole of my first year.

My first headteacher would pull me into their office and berate my skills, pick holes in my knowledge, discuss how the parents had made complaints about me, and even criticise my formality of wearing a

DOI: 10.4324/9781003317913-1

suit. I felt a failure on so many occasions. The bullying usually occurred just before the start of school, preventing me from preparing adequately, and I would be close to tears as I walked out to collect my class from the school playground. I dreaded the weekly dressing down that I went through. This went on for almost four months before one of my colleagues happened to mention that the headteacher was a known bully who picked on all the new staff. I couldn't believe what she was saying. As I was a newly qualified teacher, I had mistakenly assumed that the headteacher was correct and that I was inexperienced and unable to see things as they truly were. My colleague explained all the things that had happened to her, and I realised that they were identical to the strategies being used against me.

Over the following five months, I began to stand up for myself. I decided that I would no longer be the victim. Each time I was called into the office, I listened to what was being said, asked for more information and highlighted where it was clearly an opinion being used against me, I stood up to it. Over the months, the bullying diminished and finally ended. I had stopped being the victim, and I was no longer bullied during my many enjoyable years at this school. I also talked to all the new staff who joined and said that if they ever got bullied, this was something that was the headteacher's problem, not theirs. I refused to stand by and allow anyone else to go through the same emotional battering that I had endured.

www.blobtree.com

This book provides a set of sheets to enable victims to share their stories, to work out how to resist those who are bullying them and to regain a joy in life. It also is for all of us as bystanders, who watch others being intimidated – support them in their journey.

For those who bully, the journey is equally challenging. In my life I watched the bully turn into a victim. I never chose to take advantage of it. I couldn't help them to break free from this pattern, but what I was able to do was to protect others from being bullied. If this book helps to support victims from bullies then I will feel that it was worth it.

If you have experienced bullying and feel powerless to stop it, please talk to someone whom you can trust who will help you to escape this cycle. Bullying can happen in the workplace, at home, in a friendship or within society at large.

How To use This Book

BLOB BULLYING

Blob Bullying Feelosophy

Blobs are a way of communicating using two of the first languages which we learn as children – body language and feelings. Before we can speak, before we can write, we have all learned to read the signs in our parents' faces and appreciate being held and hugged. This means that Blobs are an all-age resource. In Ian's own school work, he has used them with children as young as four who have already begun to recognise when they feel like these 'funny people'. Blobs live in a strange world which our eyes cannot see but our heart can discern. We can learn to 'read' the world emotionally and identify who is walking around with a thundercloud over their lives or is like the sun bursting forth!

We can learn a new way of seeing – emotionally.

Blobs work best when we take the time to start with ourselves. We wouldn't dream of teaching a child to tie their laces if we hadn't learned to do it first ourselves. Likewise, we need to reflect upon our own hearts using Blobs before we encourage others to do the same. We have found that the best way to create an open atmosphere is to model openness to the groups or individuals we are working with. Work through each activity yourself or with a trusted friend before using it with your group, being willing to being vulnerable.

Talk to yourself like you would to someone you love. Brene Brown

www.blobtree.com

The more we know ourselves the more others can know us too.

The activities are suitable for individuals, small groups or large ones. We've used Blobs with groups of thousands. Start small and build up your confidence to use them effectively. Never push people to reveal more than they want to. We all need to trust the groups we are in – this can take minutes or years, depending upon how well everyone gets on. Forcing people to step out beyond their comfort boundaries can lead to the opportunity for openness to close down right at the start. It is better to model it and allow others to take a similar risk.

DOI: 10.4324/9781003317913-2

Sharing our inner selves is a risk... but one worth taking.

Kindness is such a key subject in our society and where it is absent, classes, schools, families and whole communities can feel devoid of love. The following tools are a variety of ideas to kickstart your work. There are loads more ways of using the sheets, cards and other Blob resources.

General Questions to Ask Yourself and Others about the Blob Kindness Resources

Which Blob:

1: ...would you like to sit with?

2: ...do you feel least like?

3: ...do you feel like at the start of the week?

4: ...is how you feel when you walk into your home?

5: ...is how you felt at school?

6: ...is how you felt yesterday?

7: ...is how you feel about going on holiday?

8: ...is how you feel when you wake up in the morning?

9: ...is how you feel about God?

10: ...is how you felt when you were bullied?

11: ...is most like your mother?

12: ...do you feel like at the end of the week?

13: ...confuses you?

14: ...is how you feel with children?

15: ...is how you feel when you go to bed at night?

16: ...is how you feel at a place of worship?

17: ...is how you felt at the age of 5?

18: ...is how you feel with adults?

19 ...is how you feel when you are confronted by violence?

20 ...is how you feel with animals?

21: …is when you last felt stupid?

22: …is most like your father?

23: …is how you felt at the age of 11?

24: …is how you feel about being photographed?

25: …is how you felt when you were last kissed?

26: …is how you feel going shopping?

27: …is how you feel when someone tells you off?

28: …do you feel like in a pub?

29: …is when you have to sort out an argument?

30: …is how you felt at the age of 21?

31: …is when you get angry?

32: …is when you win a competition?

33: …is your brother or sister?

34: …is when you tell a lie?

35: …is when you go to a party?

36: …is how you feel when your parents are with you?

37: …is when someone points out your mistakes?

38: …is when you have free time?

39: …is how you feel about dying?

40: …is how you feel about going to hospital?

41: …reminds you of Christmas?

42: …is how you feel under pressure?

43: …is how you feel when you are under pressure to change?

44: …is how you feel in a new group of people?

45: …is how you feel about getting older?

46: …is how you feel being with people who break the law?

Be the love you never received

www. blobtree..com

47: …do you feel like when people ask you to help them?

48: …do you feel like today?

49: …reminds you of your boss?

50: …is how you feel when driving?

51: …is how you feel when you see someone with a disability?

52: …is the Blob you've never been?

BLOB BULLYING

Questions and the Blob Pictures

'We become fully conscious only of what we are able to express to someone else.'

Paul Tournier, *The Meaning of Persons*

Questions are a very powerful tool. Those who work with people in education, law, care and personal development receive training in how to use them. A question such as, 'What can I do to solve the problem of poverty?' prompted Bob Geldof to initiate 'Live Aid' and Bono to urge the G8 leaders to end international debt. Talking about our own thoughts and feelings enables us to understand where we are and where we need to change.

Can You Think of a Question Which Changed the Direction of Your Life?

Making time to talk about things in our heart has become part of the primary National Curriculum in 'circle time'. Counsellors are skilled in the art of both asking probing questions and listening to the spoken and unspoken responses so that they can ask further questions. Job interviews depend on questions and those who are skilled in how to answer them move on in their personal ambitions.

Church ministers use them to provoke us to think about our personal beliefs. Lawyers are trained in asking pertinent questions which expose the motives behind our actions and reveal what we don't want others to know about us. We all appreciate people who want to listen to our problems and ask us the questions that give us the space to talk.

Who Asks You the Best Questions in Your Life?

The most famous people in history were skilled at asking questions: Freud used them to reveal the thoughts of his clients; Jesus used them to expose the motives of religious hypocrites; Newton used them to understand the design of the universe; Mother Teresa used them to stir up the feelings of those who came to see her work with the world's poorest people; Martin Luther King Jr. used them to challenge racist attitudes.

Are There Aspects of Your Work Which Would Be Improved by Asking More Questions?

There are different types of questions ranging from superficial ones (How you doing?) to deep and probing ones (What started you crying?). When you use the Blob pictures, remember that we all like to be questioned in a sensitive way. Sometimes we want to talk, and other times we like to listen. Start with general questions and then enquire about your group's opinions, before finally giving them the opportunity to reveal the thoughts in their hearts. This whole process can happen the first time you meet together or it can take years.

Being vulnerable is the same as being authentic and warm all humans to this

PIP WILSON

www.blobtree.com

When Did a Question Give You the Space to Come to Your Own Conclusion?

Valuing group member's response to the pictures is essential. It enables the others to discuss more freely. There are no right or wrong answers. The Blobs provide your group with a chance to talk about an issue, or about themselves, using an image rather than a set of words. For some people it may be as simple as pointing at a picture to describe themselves; for others it will start a conversation full of stories.

BLOB BULLYING

Blob Questions Menu

Not all questions are equal. Some don't threaten the listener, while others require a degree of self-revelation. Here is a basic question menu. The starters tend to be about facts relating to the Blobs. The main course is where sharing one's thoughts and opinions happen. The dessert is where the deepest answers will be required. The questions require feelings to be shared. Don't rush this process. Some people take a long time to open up and share their opinions. Often, what they are wanting is an example from the leader of being vulnerable, so they can see how the group responds.

Add your own; these are just to start you off.

Starters (general questions)

Which Blobs look happy?

Which Blobs look sad?

Find a Blob that interests you.

Which Blob looks cool?

Which Blob looks like a child?

Which Blob looks lonely?

Main Course (exploring opinions)

Which Blob is the most positive?

Which Blob is the most negative?

Which Blob reminds you of your boss?

Which Blob cares the most?

Which Blob do you not understand?

Which Blob could be the leader?

Which Blob is definitely female?

Which Blob is definitely male?

Which Blob is likely to be in trouble with the police?

Which Blob is working for the police?

Which Blob is rich?

Which Blob is most likely to be taking drugs?

Which Blob could die soon?

Which Blob could God be?

Which Blob could God not be?

Dessert (exploring feelings)

Which Blob or Blobs do you feel like? Why?

Which Blob would you like to be? Why?

Which Blob do you feel like when you've been drinking? Why?

Which Blob scares you? Why?

Which Blob reminds you of your mum? Why?

Which Blob reminds you of your dad? Why?

Which Blob is the friend you've always wanted? Why?

Which Blob would you keep away from? Why?

Which Blob annoys you the most? Why?

The fear of bullying is exhausting!

www.blobtree.com

Blob Bullying Worksheets

Stages of Bullying

Look at the Stages of Bullying picture with a talk partner – discuss what you see.

Can you give a word to describe the types of bullying the Blobs are displaying?

Which Blobs are the victims, in your opinion?

Which types of bullying do you find easy to recognise?

Identify one type of bullying which you find a challenge.

www.blobtree.com

The stages of bullying

Stop Bullying

Coping Mechanisms

Effects of Bullying

Fueling the Negative Reaction

Identifying Victims

Bullying Begins

www.blobtree.com

THE BLOB GUIDE TO

BLOB BULLYING

Blob Victims

Look at the Blob Victims picture with a talk partner – discuss what you see.

Which Blob is the most likely to be a victim, in your opinion?

What reason can you imagine that each Blob could be bullied for?

Which Blob have you seen being a victim?

Which Blobs have you ever felt like?

Anxiety is a state of constant choices

www.blobtree.com

Copyright material from Pip Wilson and Ian Long (2023), *Blob Bullying*, Routledge

Blob Victims?

www.blobtree.com

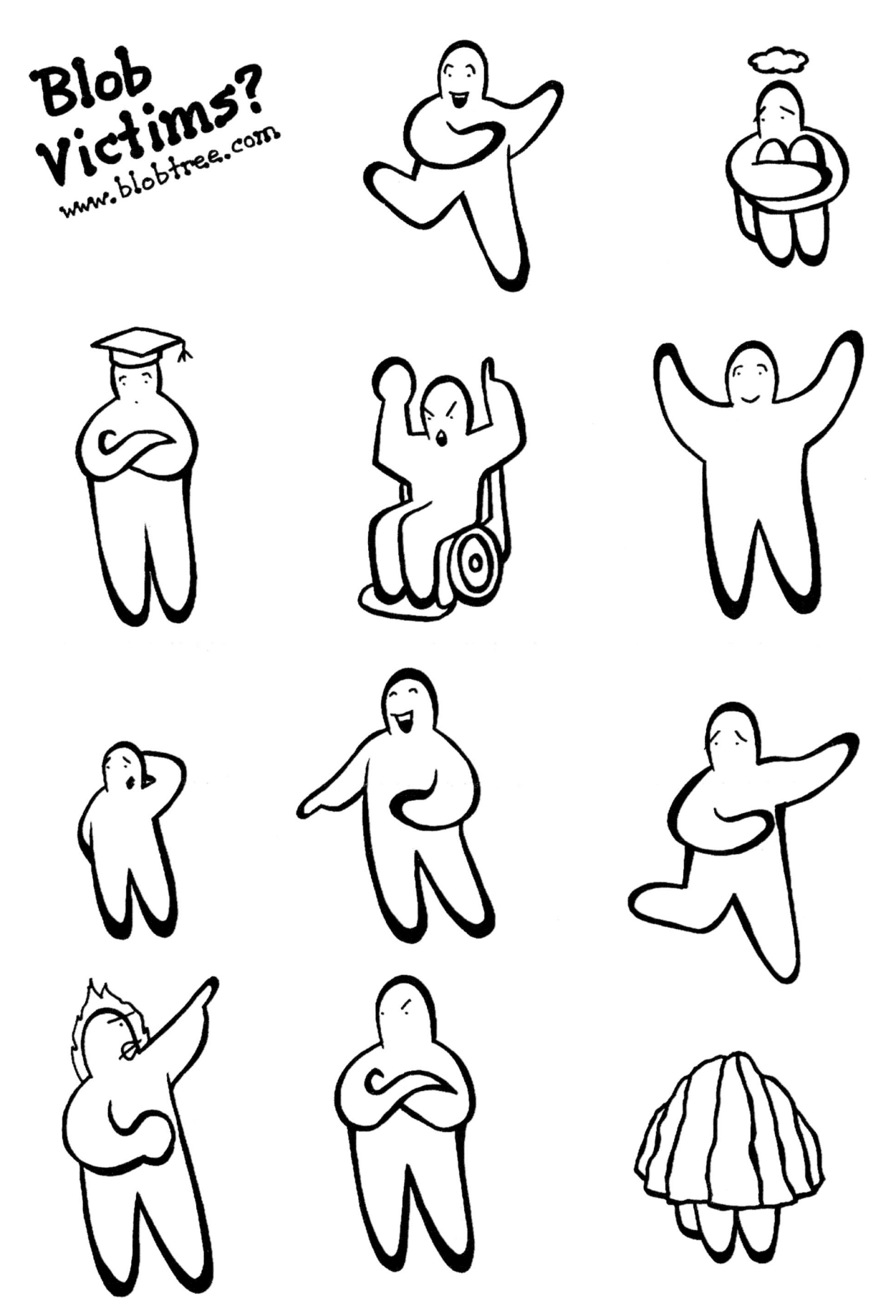

THE BLOB GUIDE TO

BLOB BULLYING

Blob Bullying Tree

Look at the Blob Bullying Tree picture with a talk partner – discuss what you see.

Which Blobs are the victims, in your opinion?

Can you give a word to describe the types of bullying the Blobs are experiencing?

Which types of bullying do you find easy to recognise?

Identify one type of bullying which you find a challenge.

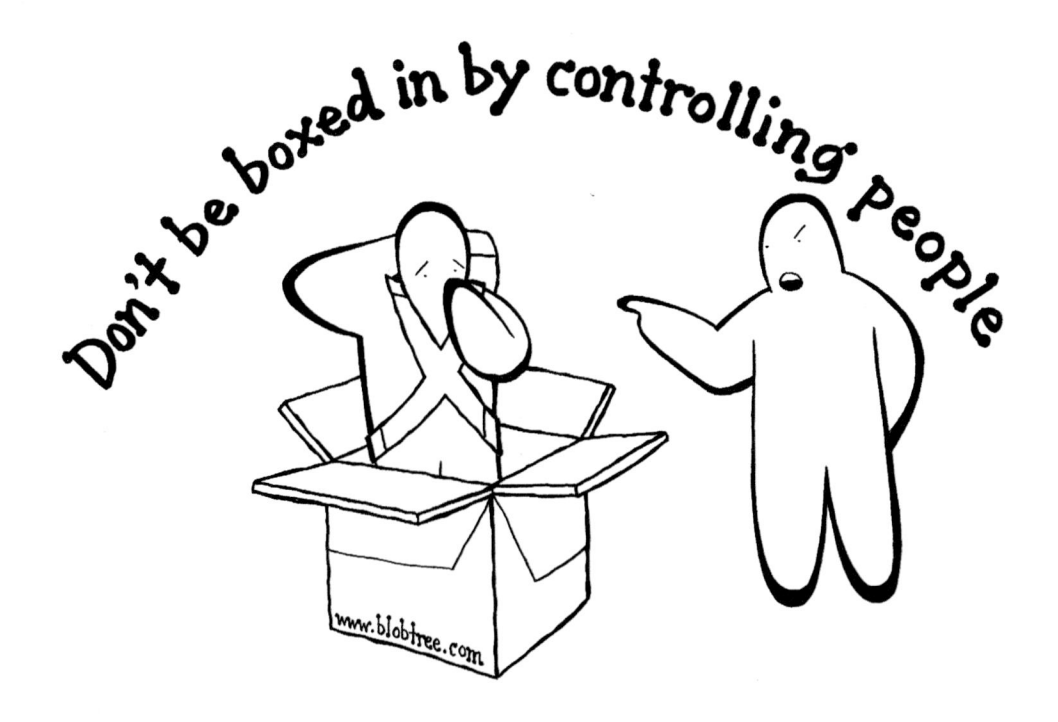

THE BLOB GUIDE TO

BLOB BULLYING

Blob Kindness Tree

Look at the Blob Kindness Tree picture with a talk partner – discuss what you see.

How is each Blob being kind?

Which types of kindness have you experienced this week?

Which type of kindness do you enjoy carrying out?

Which type of kindness would you like to try?

When things change inside me... ... things change around me www.blobtree.com

BLOB BULLYING

Blob Unkind Tree

Look at the Blob Unkind Tree with a talk partner – discuss what you see.

How is each Blob being unkind?

Which types of unkindness have you experienced this week?

Which type of unkindness is the worst?

Which Blob would you keep well away from?

THE BLOB GUIDE TO
BLOB BULLYING

Blob Human Rights Tree

Human rights were set up to protect each and every individual from abuses across the world. By protecting every person, we protect humanity collectively.

Look at the Blob Human Rights Tree picture with a talk partner – discuss what you see.

Which Blobs are having problems with their rights?

Which Blobs are trying to protect others? How?

Which Blob would you choose to help first? Why?

THE BLOB GUIDE TO
BLOB BULLYING

Blob Numbered Tree

Look at the Blob Numbered Tree picture with a talk partner – discuss what you see.

Give each Blob a feeling word.

Which feelings have you felt recently?

Which feelings do you often experience from others?

Which feelings do you rarely encounter?

THE BLOB GUIDE TO
BLOB BULLYING

Gaslighting Sheets

Look at these sheets one at a time with a talk partner – discuss what you see. Only use one in a whole session. Focus first on gaslighting behaviours and finish with effective strategies to cope with this extreme form of bullying.

First sheet: An extreme form of bullying – gaslighting

What types of Gaslighting do you think is the worst?

What feelings do you imagine the bully and victim are feeling?

Which of these types of behaviour have you seen or experienced?

Second sheet: Effective strategies to deal with gaslighting

Which of these strategies would be quick and easy to put in place?

Which of these strategies would be best done gradually?

Which of these strategies have you found to be effective?

Have you found any other strategies to be effective?

Our individual human rights protect us from powerful tyrants

www.blobtree.com

Gaslighting

An extreme form of bullying

www.blobtree.com

Actions do not match words

Occasionally praises you – confusing

People are united against you and describe you as crazy

Attacks your record instead

Denies saying things

Projects their problems onto you

Telling blatant lies

Wears you out

Confusion weakens people

Recognise how you respond to the bully

Find people who can both support and advise you

If they won't change, leave for your own sanity + safety

Research their strategies

Study their tactics

Effective Strategies to deal with

Gaslighting

www.blobtree.com

Ignore the anger + avoid arguing with their reality

You are a beautiful human Person - no matter what the bully says

Withdraw for your own health + go to a friend

Set clear boundaries

My Feelings Diary

Look at the My Feelings Diary picture with a talk partner – discuss what you see.

Which feelings do you often experience?

Which feelings have you felt so far today?

You might like to track your feelings over a period of days, using a different colour for each day.

High/Low

www.blobtree.com

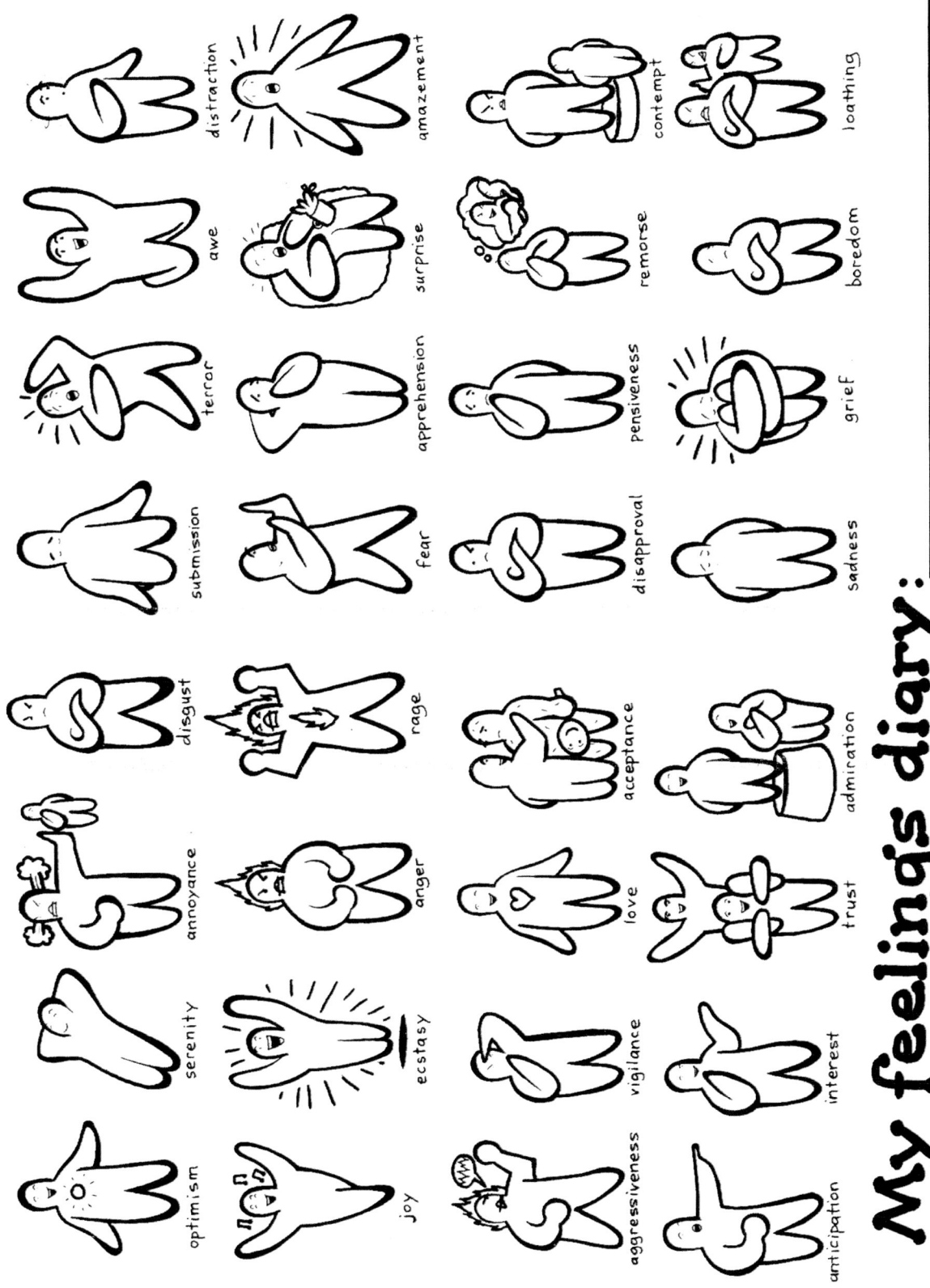

BLOB BULLYING

Blob Mood Detector

Look at the Blob Mood Detector picture with a talk partner – discuss what you see.

The picture shows four sectors – anger, joy, sadness/loneliness and calmness.

Which feelings do you often experience?

Which feelings have you felt so far today?

Which feelings do you rarely experience?

You might like to track your feelings over a period of days, using a different colour for each day. Do your feelings tend to be in certain mood sectors of the picture?

Blob Mood Detector

www.blobtree.com

Blob Drawing the Line.

Drawing the Line

The following section is a set of visual tools which enable pupils of all abilities to participate by simply using a circle, tick, underline or cross. Each image is a visual scale from one extreme to another, e.g. in the 'Listening' image one end depicts talking without listening, while the other end depicts listening thoughtfully. The three questions below are examples of topics which may be used with this scale. When I used to share these with others, such as parents or fellow staff, I always included the questions for their reference. Before I allowed the pupils to make their mark, I would model possible reasons why I would choose certain Blobs. For those less certain of what the scale represented, it gave them a rough idea of where their feelings or experiences lay.

Circle the Blob that has an unhealthy amount of anger.
Underline the Blob that you have felt like recently.
Tick the Blob that shows the amount of anger you have experienced from a bully.

DOI: 10.4324/9781003317913-3

Victim

Circle the Blob that shows how bullying feels.

Underline the Blob that has been bullied only a few times.

Tick the Blob that you felt like as a child.

Bystander

Circle the Blob that is being a helpful bystander.

Underline the Blob that is being an unhelpful bystander.

Tick the Blob that you tend to be after noticing bullying.

Angrr!

Circle the Blob that shows your first memory of anger.

Underline the Blob that feels like now.

Tick the Blob that shows how a bully treated you.

Anxiety

Circle the Blob that shows a common amount of anxiety.

Underline the Blob that you feel like when meeting someone new.

Tick the Blob that shows how you feel coming to work/school.

Bullying

Circle the Blob that is how you felt at the worst point of your bullying.

Underline the Blob that is how you felt at the start of a relationship/job.

Tick the Blob that you feel like today.

Isolation

Circle the Blob that shows how lonely you feel at school/work.

Underline the Blob that shows how lonely you feel at home.

Tick the Blob that shows how you feel with your best friend.

Depression

Circle the Blob that has been bullied for a long time.

Underline the Blob that you felt like recently.

Tick the Blob that you feel like at the weekend.

Overwhelmed

Circle the Blob that you have felt like at the start of most days.

Underline the Blob that you feel like when you are most overwhelmed.

Tick the Blob that you feel like now.

Self-acceptance

Circle the Blob that is happy with themself.

Underline the Blob that was bullied yesterday.

Tick the Blob that you feel like right now.

Self-confidence

Circle the Blob that has recently asked for help about bullying.

Underline the Blob that has been bullied for years.

Tick the Blob that has never been bullied.

Blob
Bullying
Cards

BLOB BULLYING

Ways to Use These Blob Bullying Cards

This set of photocopiable cards explore a wide range of images depicting feelings that have been described by victims of bullying. They are taken from the breadth of experiences of victim, bystander and bully, and include visual strategies for managing feelings.

Here are twenty card activities which you might try with those who you are working with:

1. Lay out a wide range of cards. Ask the individual you are working with to create a story of their day by selecting appropriate images from the pack.
2. Ask the person you are working with to think of a few words to describe each Blob card. If they are unsure, put them in one pile, and if they can describe the image, place the card in a separate pile. Go through the named pile and sort out the feelings that they have experienced themselves as having.
3. Provide a chosen set of cards and ask them to create a scale of feelings from the least intense to the most intense.

4. Place all the cards face up and ask the person to select a few which they have felt at a specific time, such as recently/at night time/on the way to school/on the way home/over the weekend etc.
5. Provide the individual with the strategies for managing the bullying. Sort them into three piles – effective and ineffective, as well as untried.
6. Ask the individual to find Blob cards that they felt like at the start of their experience of bullying.
7. Sort out the Blobs into piles of bully, victim and undecided.
8. Ask the individual to select three cards which summarise how their experience feels.
9. Create a 'picture of me' by choosing five Blob cards that they have felt most like in the last week.
10. Face all the cards up, and ask them to turn over all or the top three feelings that they want to go away.
11. Choose one Blob and ask the individual you are working with to write all the words that you can think about them, all the times you felt like them and what you would like to say to help them when they feel like that.
12. Ask them to choose all the Blob cards that would make them feel like it has been a good day. Discuss any unusual choices with open questions, e.g. why did you choose this card?

DOI: 10.4324/9781003317913-4

13. Ask the person you are working with to choose all the Blob cards that would make it feel like a bad day. Discuss any unusual choices.

14. The individual should choose two cards that they feel are opposites and describe the differences.

15. Ask the person to select one Blob card that feels like them for most of the day.

16. Then ask them to select one Blob that they feel guilty feeling like.

17. Ask the person you are working with to select three cards which is how their friends see them.

18. Play 'Make a Friend' by asking the individual to choose four Blob cards that would make a friend from the cards. Discuss the choices.

19. Which Blob cards scare the individual? Sort them into a small pile. Why do they scare them?

20. Ask the person you are working with to choose two cards to depict how they currently feel and two Blobs that they would like to feel like. What changes do they need to make to achieve this?

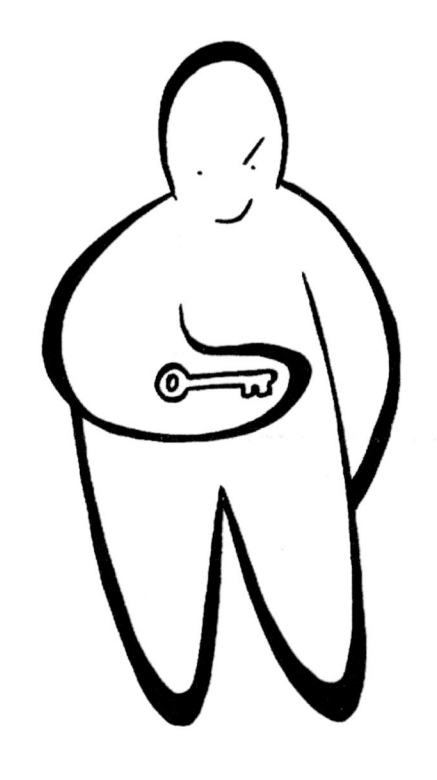

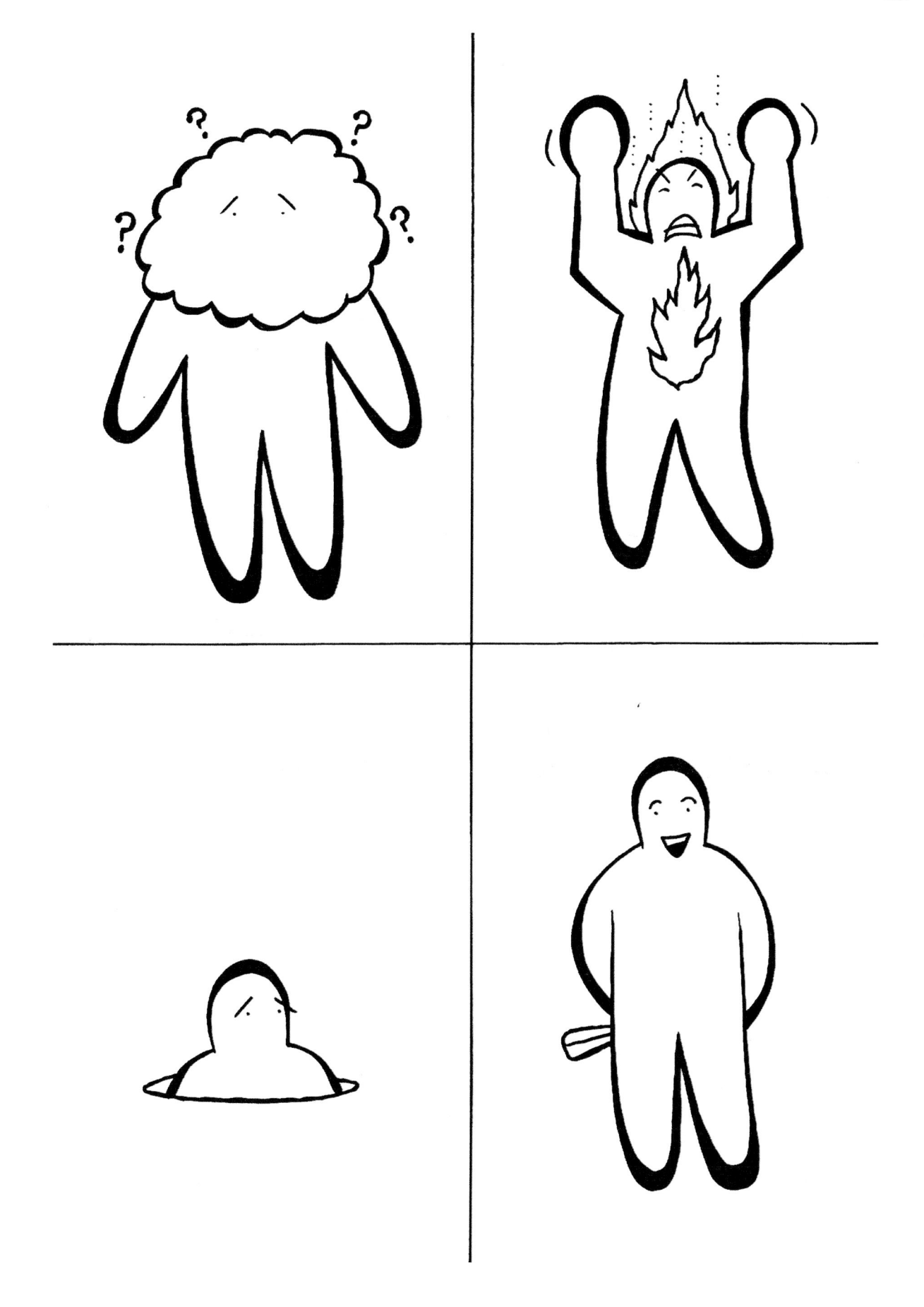

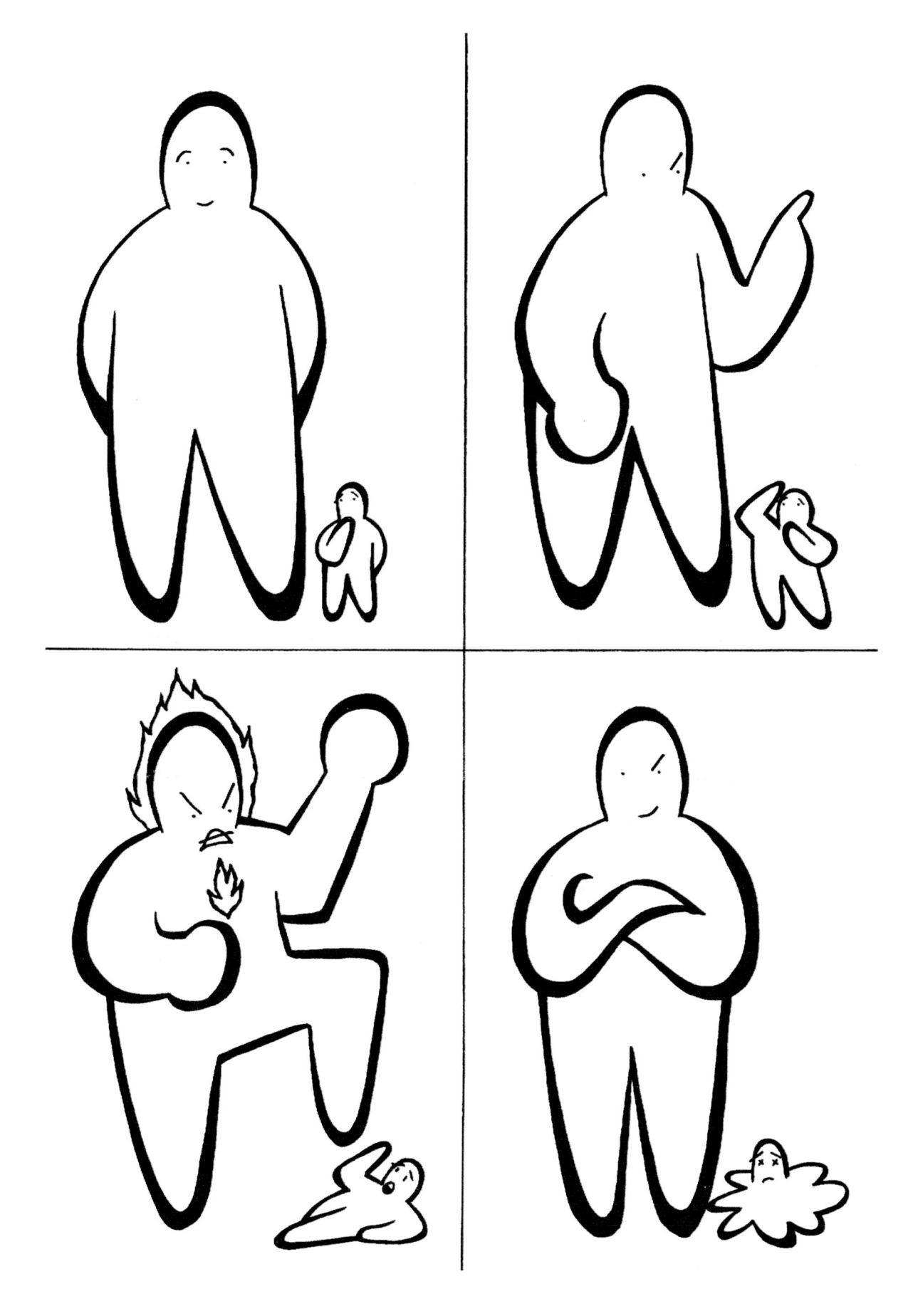

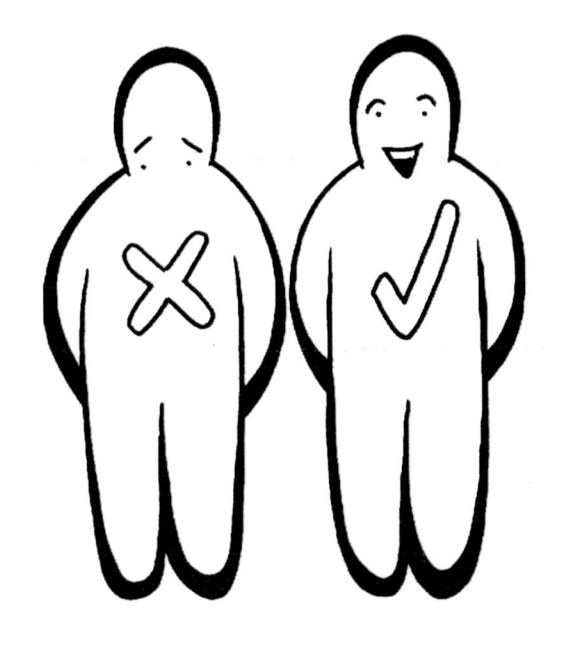

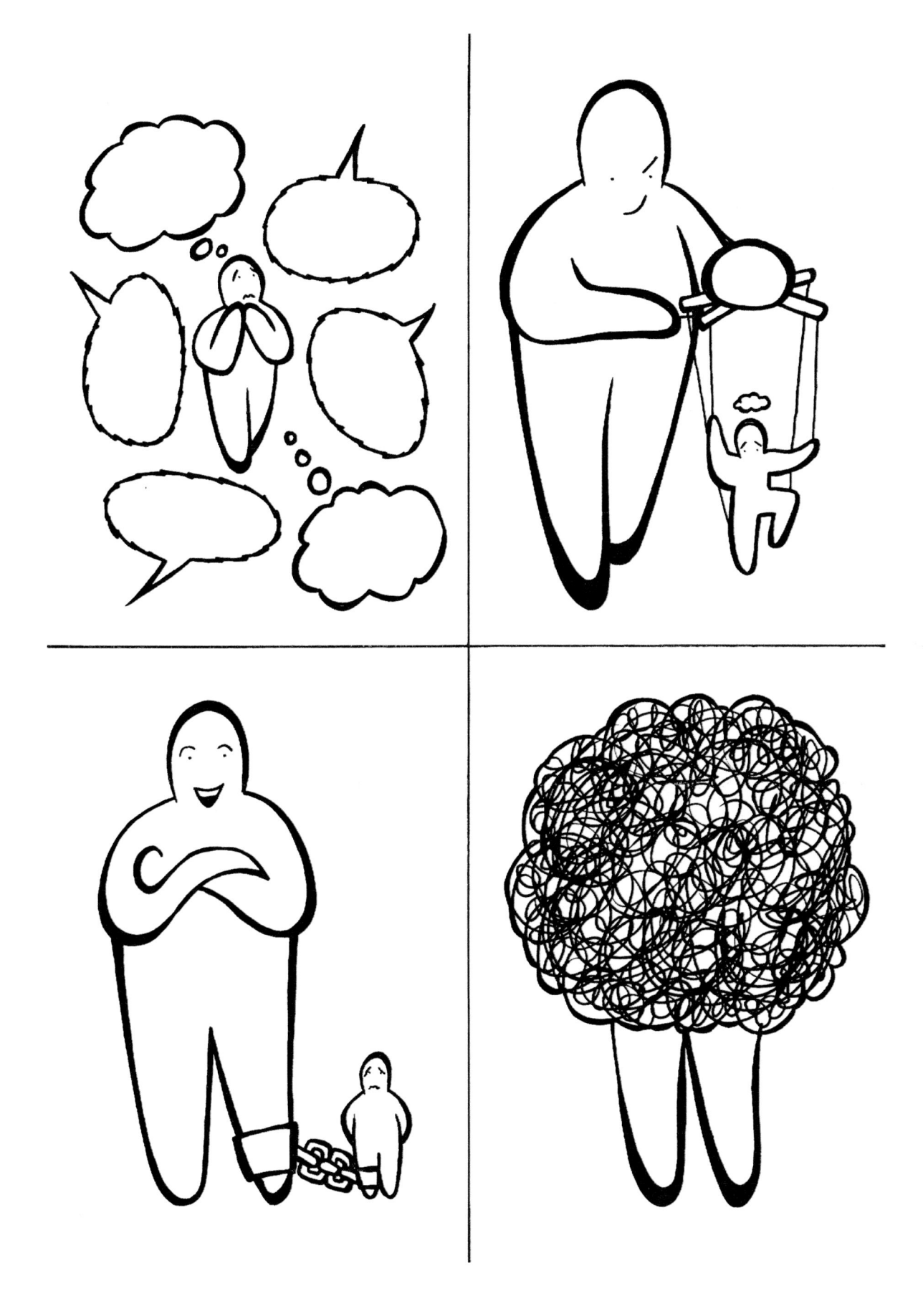

THE BLOB GUIDE TO

BLOB BULLYING

Blob Abuse

Look at the Blob Abuse picture with a talk partner – discuss what you see.

What types of abuse can you see happening to the Blobs?

Give each Blob a feelings word.

Which Blob would you support out of these different situations? Why?

Which types of abuse have you seen recently?

BLOB BULLYING

Blob Bullying

Look at the Blob Bullying picture with a talk partner – discuss what you see.

What types of bullying can you see happening to the Blobs?

Choose a cluster of Blobs and give each one a feelings word.

Which type of bullying do you find hardest to spot? Why?

Which types of bullying have you seen recently?

David
v
Goliath
2.0

www.blobtree.com

THE BLOB GUIDE TO

BLOB BULLYING

Blob Caged

This is a personal reflective tool to remind ourselves that when we are feeling isolated from others, our ability to deal with bullying is greatly reduced. However, we can connect with others, which not only gives us people who will listen to our concerns, but will act as a support when future problems occur.

Feel free to use this as a poster to be coloured in or as a visual support for victims in your workplace.

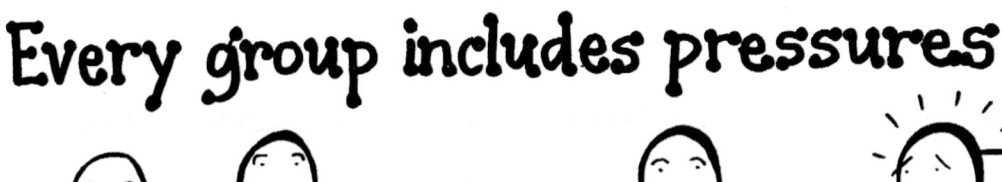

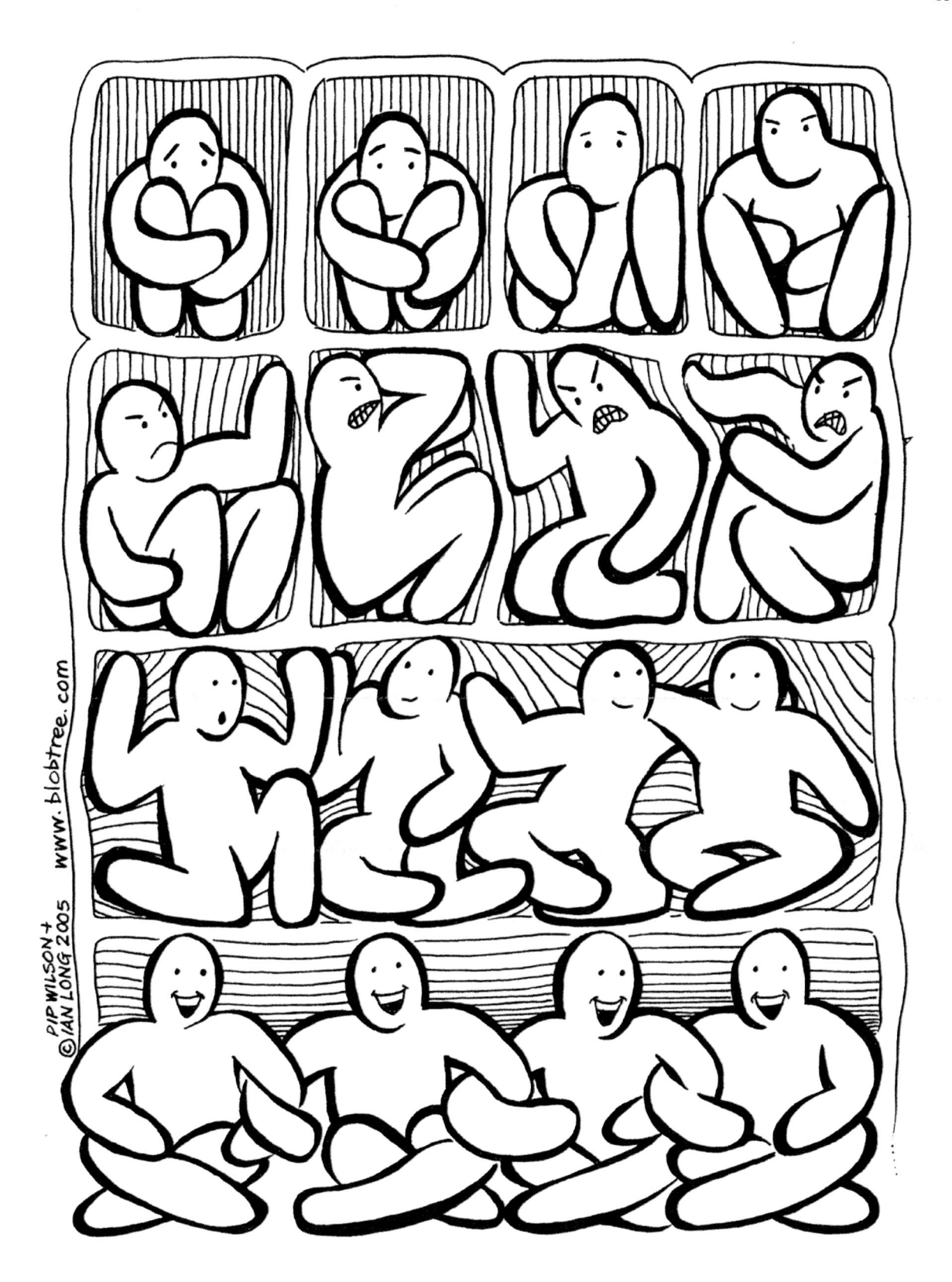

PIP WILSON + www.blobtree.com
© IAN LONG 2005

BLOB BULLYING

Blob Unkind Classroom

Look at the Blob Classroom Un/Kindness picture with a talk partner – discuss what you see.

What types of unkindness can you see happening to the Blobs?

Give each Blob a feelings word.

Which Blob would you support out of these different situations? Why?

Which types of unkindness have you seen recently?

www.blobtree.com

Copyright material from Pip Wilson and Ian Long (2023), *Blob Bullying*, Routledge

Blob Unkind Playground

Look at the Blob Unkind Playground picture with a talk partner – discuss what you see.

What types of unkindness can you see happening to the Blobs?

Give each Blob a feelings word.

Which Blob did you feel like in the school playground?

Which Blob would you support out of these different situations? Why?

Which types of unkindness have you seen recently?

BLOB UNKiND PLAYGROUND
www.blobtree.com

THE BLOB GUIDE TO
BLOB BULLYING

Blob Online Dangers

Look at the Blob Online Dangers picture with a talk partner – discuss what you see.

What types of activities can you see happening to the Blobs?

Give each Blob a feelings word.

Which Blob would you support out of these different situations? Why?

Which types of online dangers have you heard of recently?

www.blobtree.com

Copyright material from Pip Wilson and Ian Long (2023), *Blob Bullying*, Routledge

72

BLOB BULLYING

The Cycle of Revenge

Look at the Cycle of Revenge picture with a talk partner – discuss what you see.

Which stages do you think would be the hardest to pass through? Why?

What stages of revenge have you seen or experienced?

What stages of forgiveness have you seen or experienced?

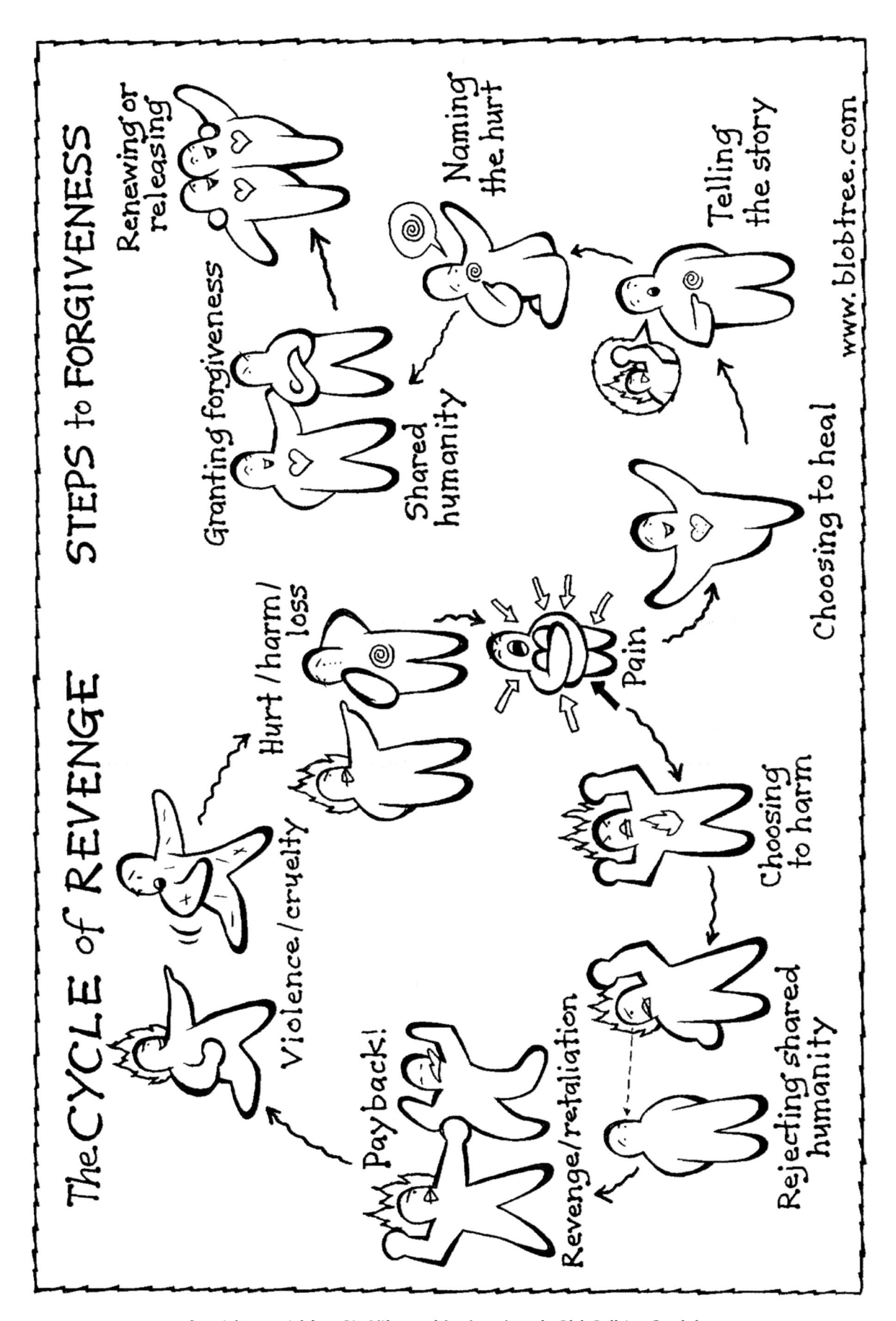

Copyright material from Pip Wilson and Ian Long (2023), *Blob Bullying*, Routledge

BLOB BULLYING

Blob Relationship

Look at the Blob Relationship picture with a talk partner – discuss what you see.

These relationships can be applied to a partner, a friend, a colleague, etc.

Which Blobs look as if they are enjoying their relationship?

What types of relationships do you feel are unhealthy? Why?

Which type of relationships have you experienced?

Which type of relationship did you enjoy most?

Blob Bingo

BLOB BULLYING

Activity 1 – spot the Blobs' feelings. *This emotional literacy activity can be played with general feelings and more specific feelings. The more it is played, the more able the child will become at recognising their own feelings and that of those they mingle with. This is a good starting activity for each session with a child.*

Give the children a general board to look at, with the feelings words underneath the images. If they find it difficult to read the words, go through the names of the eight feelings together a couple of times. Then place the eight tiles upside down on the table and get them to guess out loud which tile they might be turning over. If they get it correct, they can put the tile on their sheet. If not, they must turn the tile over and choose another one until they find the Blob feeling that they wanted. Having done the first, they can then choose a second feeling. This continues until all the tiles have been chosen.

Activity 2 – general questions to ask. *Always choose age-appropriate questions – the list in the Blob Questions Menu at the beginning of the book is for the full age range of children. Always try to develop their choices by asking, 'Why?'*

Activity 3 – top three feelings. *An activity to make children think about which feelings they experience the most at school, home and in the playground. Always try to develop their choices by asking, 'Why?'*

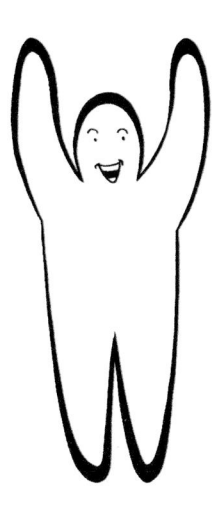

Get the child to place all the tiles on the general board to cover the Blobs' feelings. Ask them to remove from the board any feelings which they have never felt. If they are common feelings, check to see if they have felt them in a variety of situations. Some children only remember their current set of feelings. Then ask them to turn over how they are feeling now, but keep it on the board. Ask them to turn over the feeling they have at home time. Then ask the child to turn over how they felt at playtime. Ask them to remove all the tiles that they haven't turned over. The three facing down can be turned over now as their three top feelings. Do they agree or do they think that they need to add one more?

Activity 4 – spot the Blobs' body language. *This activity helps children to recognise the body language of the Blobs.*

Get the child to match the tiles to the board at the start of the activity. Get them to listen to your description of each Blob's face and body language. Explain that you won't mention the colour or feeling

DOI: 10.4324/9781003317913-5

name. If they want to make a guess, they need to say the name of the feeling after you have finished your description. If they get it correct, they can turn the Blob tile over. If you want to develop their skills further, reverse the game so that they now describe the facial and body language!

Activity 5 – which two? *Always choose age-appropriate questions – the following are for the full age range of children. Always try to develop children's choices by asking, 'Why?'*

Provide the children with the full set of eight tiles on the table. Ask them a question and then get them to select two tiles as their answer. Here are some to get you started. Make up questions relevant to the interests and needs of the child to add to this list.

Which two Blobs would you like as your friends?

Which two Blobs would work hard in the classroom?

Which two Blobs remind you of your friends?

Which two Blobs would you find difficult to be friends with?

Which two Blobs are waking-up feelings?

Which two Blobs are at school feelings?

Which two Blobs have you not felt like in your whole life?

Which two Blobs would please the teacher or parent most?

Which two Blobs would it be fun to be like?

Activities with the Five Specific Feelings Boards (Angry, Happy, Lonely, Sad, and Worried)

Activity 6 – looking at a range of one feeling. *This activity helps children to realise that each board is a scale from a weaker feeling to a stronger feeling. This helps them to move the discussion beyond one word for each emotion.*

Choose one of the boards. Anger is probably the easiest to do this with. Ask the child to find the Blob who is the least angry and the Blob who is the angriest. Establish that this board is a scale from not very angry to very angry. Go through the vocabulary together. Ask the child to order the tiles in the same order in a line.

This activity can be done for each separate board.

Activity 7 – self-awareness of one feeling. *This activity should only be done after Activity 6. It can take as long as you feel is necessary.*

Choose one of the specific emotion boards. Remind the child that this is a range of the same feeling. Get them to indicate which is the strongest feeling and which is the weakest, once more, as a reminder. Ask them to lay out the tiles over the board. Tell them that this game is to turn all of the Blobs over by thinking of a time when they might have felt like each of these feelings. Give them prompts, such as when you were angry in the playground, in the classroom, etc. This promotes self-awareness of this specific emotion. If it would help, start with a positive sheet, such as happiness. This activity can be repeated on a frequent basis as a week is a long time in the life of a child.

Activity 8 – looking at how to change a strong emotion. *This activity helps children to change their feelings when they start to feel worried, sad, angry or lonely.*

Choose one of the four boards pertinent to the child. Discuss which Blob they have felt like recently. Ask them what made them feel that way. What time of day was it? Who were they with? These three factors may be reoccurring themes that set off their feelings. Ask them how they stopped feeling like it? What changed their feeling back to normal? Get them to line up the feelings in reverse from the strongest to the weakest. Ask the child to add one of the happy images which they like. If they haven't found a method to calm themselves down, use one of the following which they feel might work: talking to a friend, using a stress ball, counting to ten, deep breathing, asking an adult for help.

How do we
respond
to big
issues
?

www.blobtree.com

lonely

confused

sad

trusting

happy

worried

angry

shy

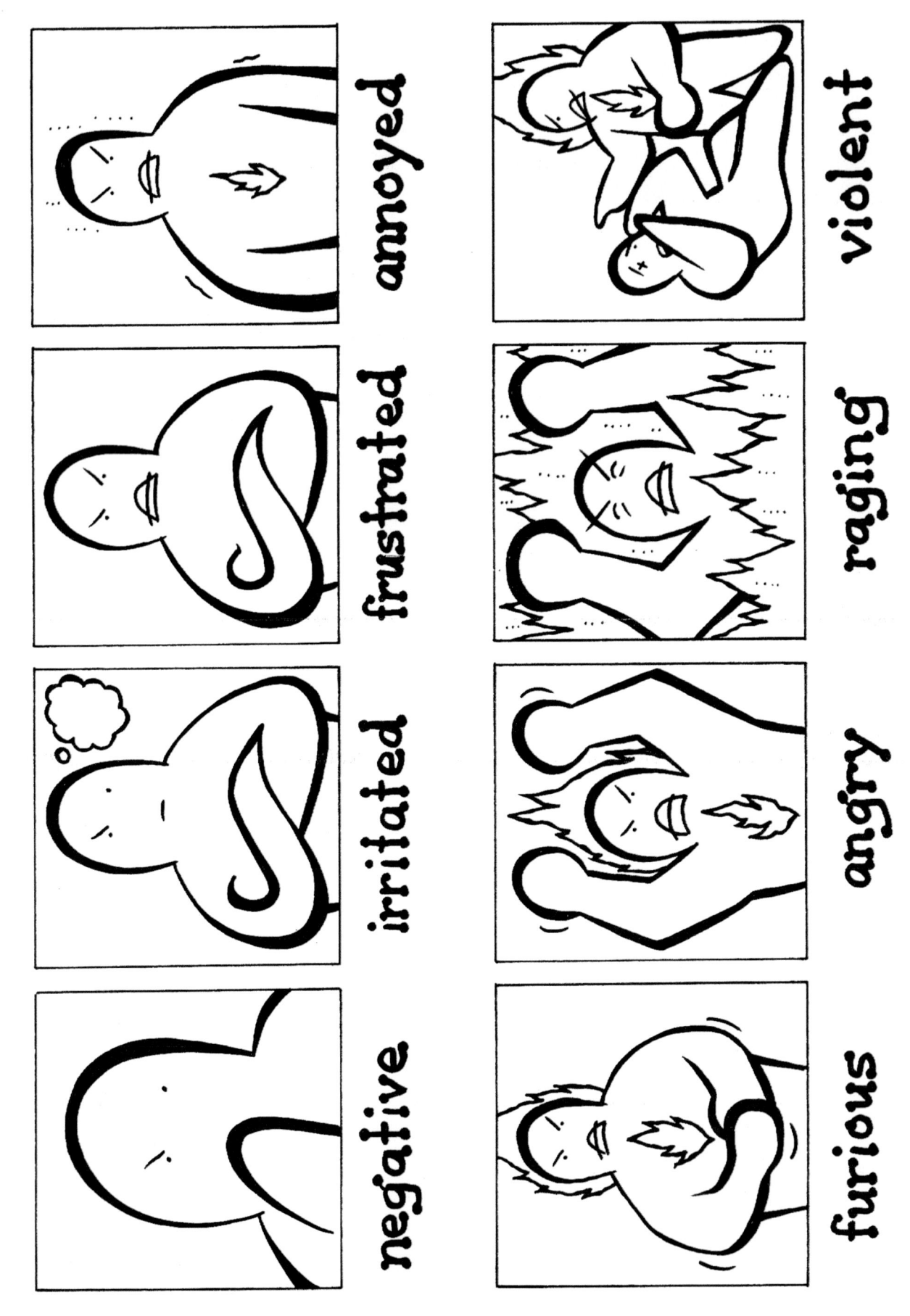

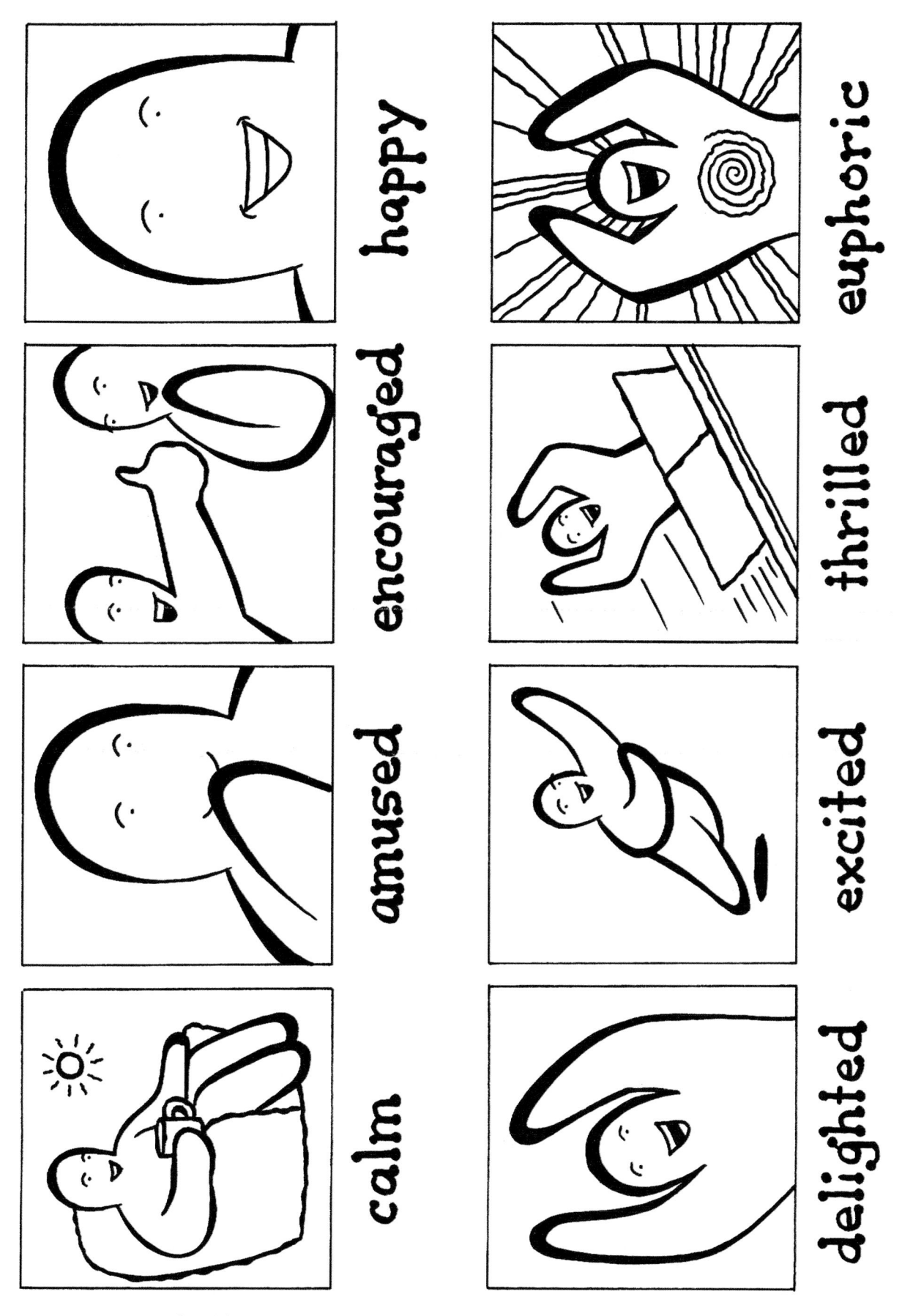

happy

euphoric

encouraged

thrilled

amused

excited

calm

delighted

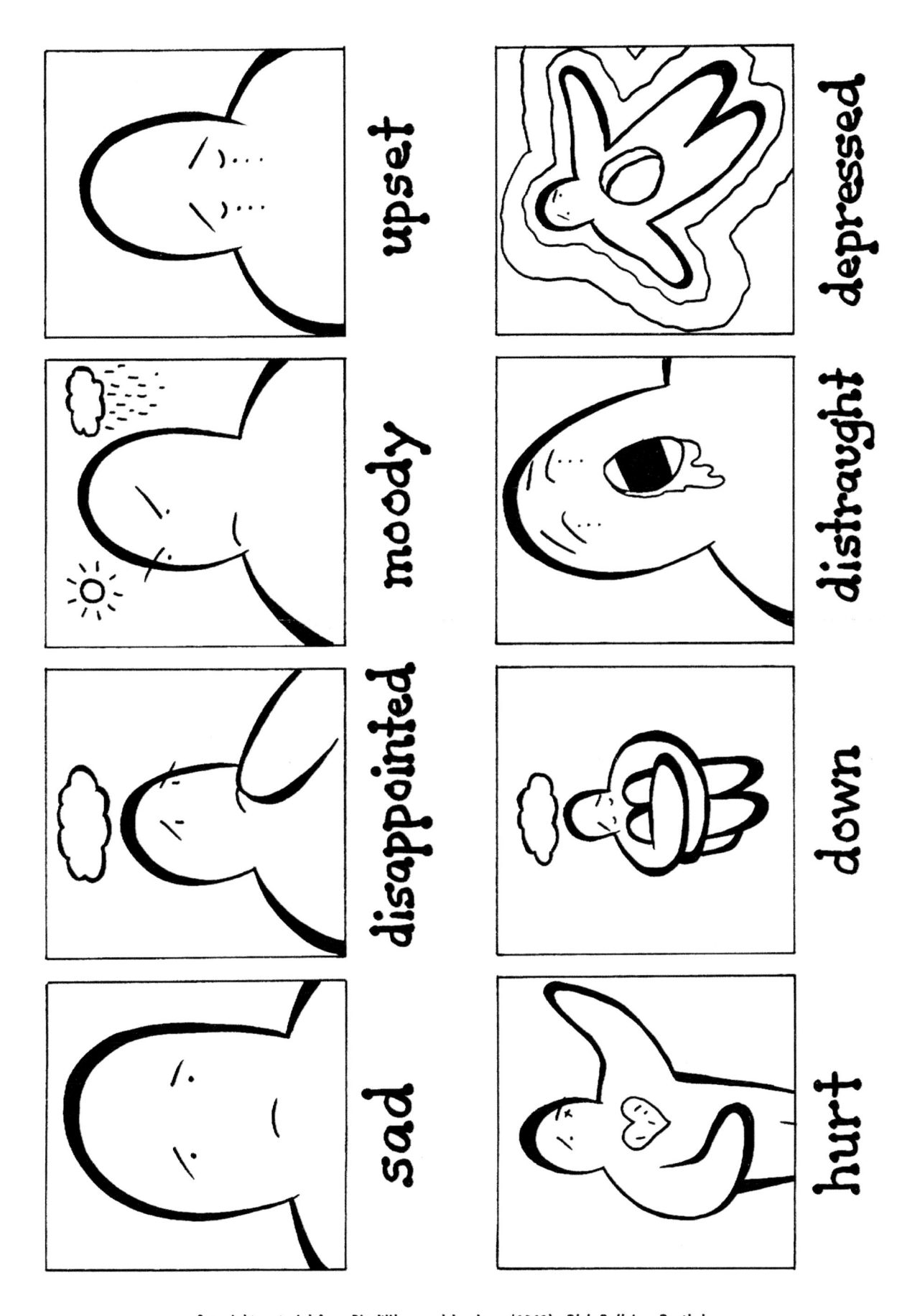

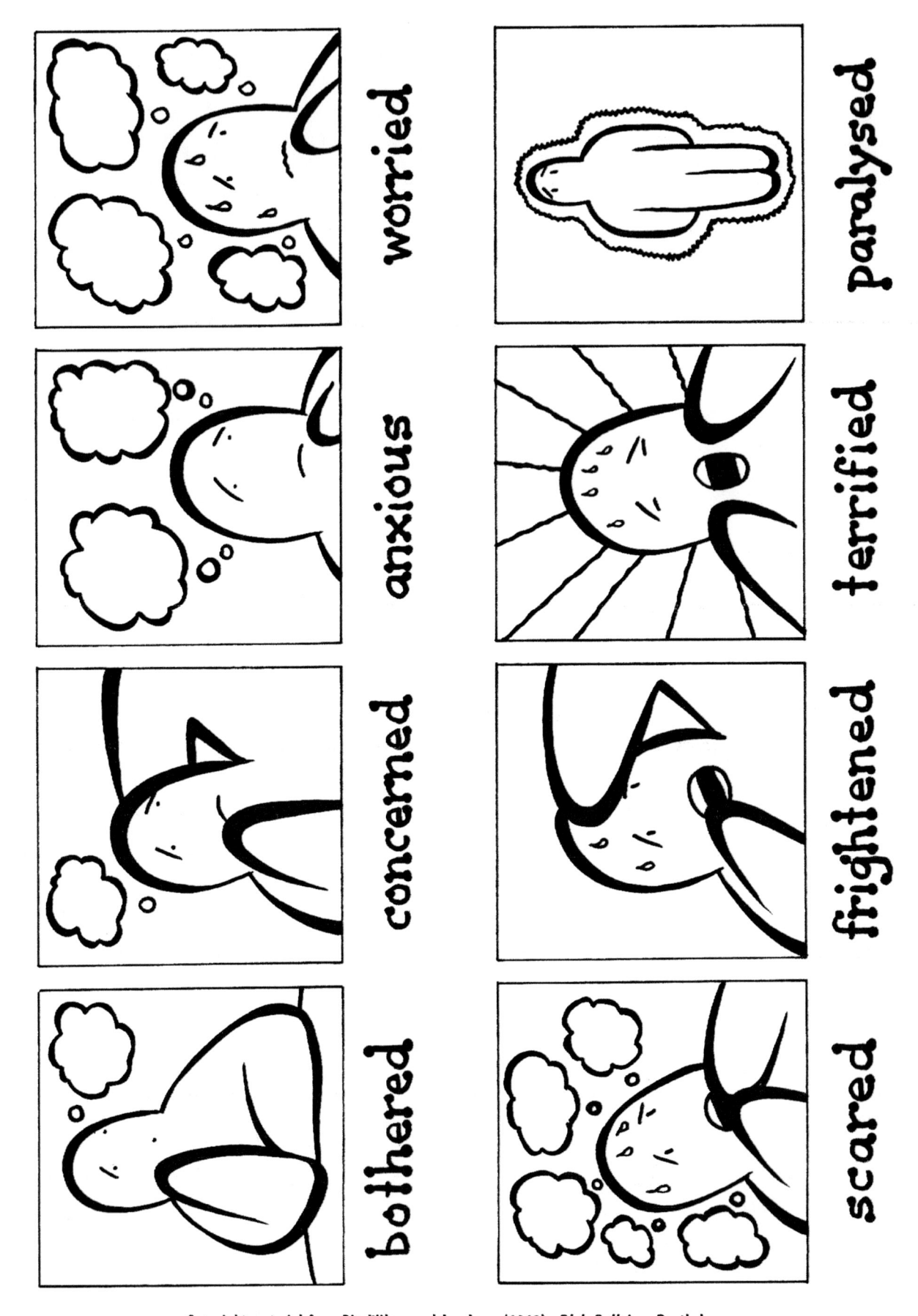

Blob Bullying Situations

BLOB BULLYING

The three following visual tools are for discussing the situations where bullying might have occurred. Sometimes events take place in a school setting, sometimes at home, and the third scenario is an imaginary place of boxes and hiding places to accommodate any other situations.

The individual discussing the bullying might find it easier to select a Blob for both themselves and the bully. That way, the characters can be moved around the scenario to depict what has occurred. Sometimes, in the act of moving, the experience can be acted out in a way that words cannot convey.

This tool needs to be handled carefully to avoid suggesting ideas to a child or impressionable adult. These visual aids are a means to release conversation and need to be used by someone familiar with helping individuals to express their feelings and experiences. As such, they need to be used alongside conversation, questioning and other methods of clarification.

As well as acting out what has happened, the individual may wish to select a Blob to act out how to deal with the situation in a better way. They may need help to develop new skills in this way and to talk through the feelings associated with their behaviour.

Constantly retreating to our safe space makes our world smaller + brings fear closer + closer to home

www.blobtree.com

DOI: 10.4324/9781003317913-6

BLOB PLAYGROUND

© Pip Wilson + Ian Long

www.blobtree.com

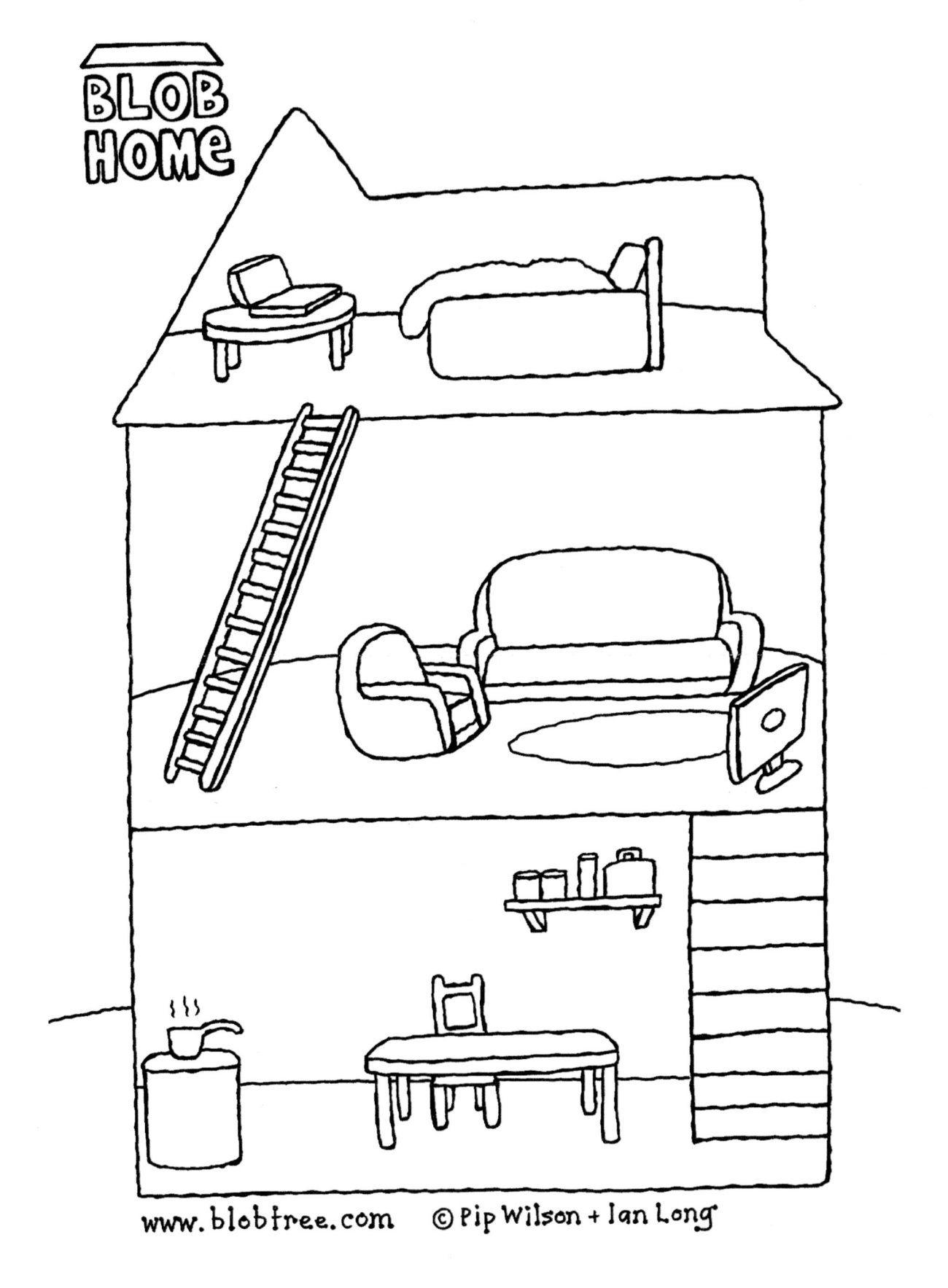

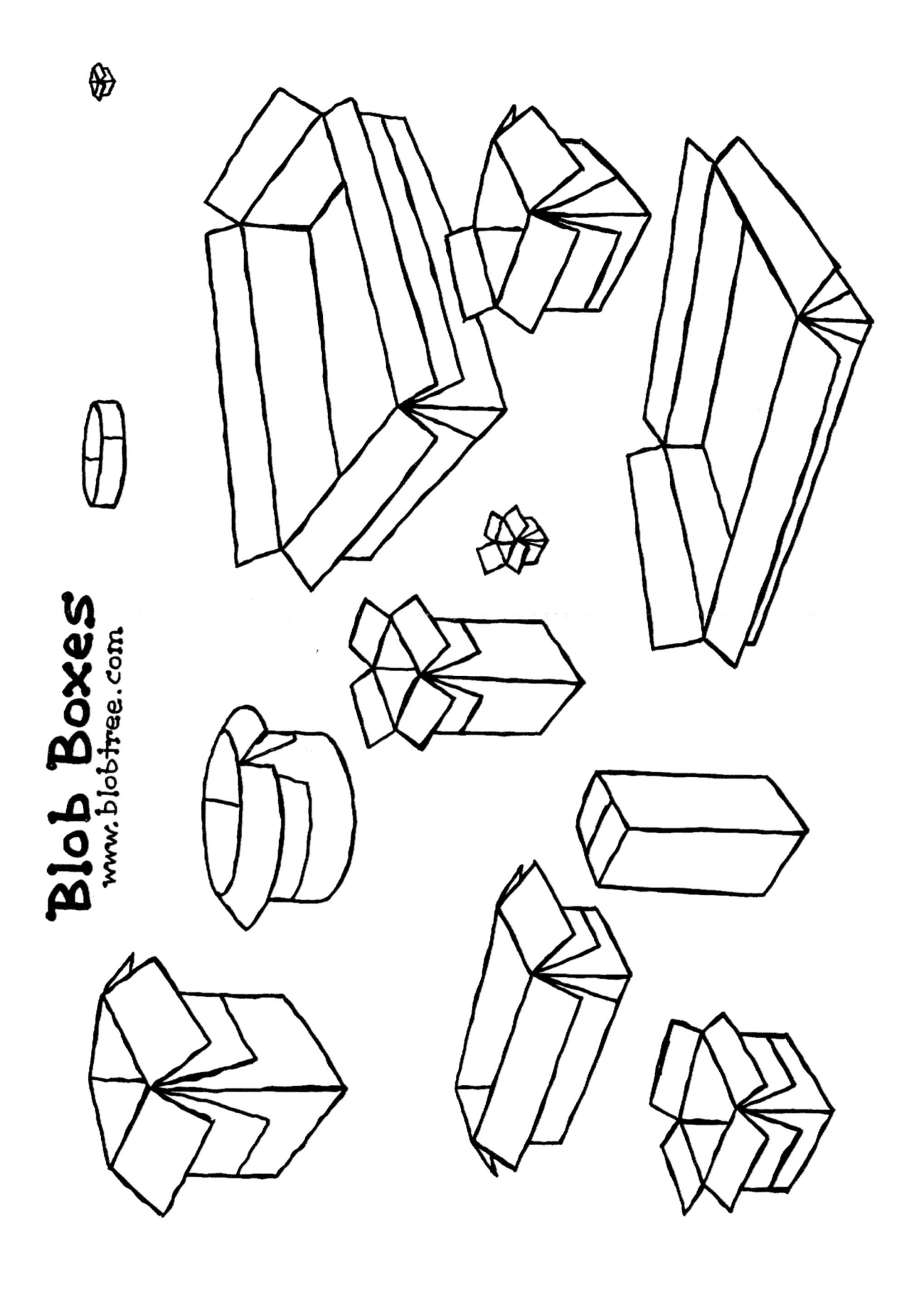

Blob Boxes
www.blobtree.com

Blob
Control
Sheets

BLOB BULLYING

Blob Control Discussion Starter Sheets

The following pages are a series of images based around the idea of one individual controlling another, which has been symbolised by a box – the idea of being boxed in. We have seen this happening many times in relationships – sometimes this can occur in family dynamics, in friendships and in couples of all ages. When using these images with words, allow time for people to read through the various images, to discuss what they might represent, how what they represent could be positive or negative, and why people sometimes choose to be boxed in within a friendship or relationship. One way of introducing this with a group could be as follows:

Give out sheets one between two for pairs to look at and discuss. After a while, you might like to ask for feedback or ask the following questions.

Which Blobs are being controlled? Which Blobs are controlling?

Which of these images depict a positive scenario?

Which of these Blobs have you felt like at home, school, work or in a friendship?

What would you say to the Blob that is standing in the box?

What would you say to the Blob that is controlling the other Blob?

DOI: 10.4324/9781003317913-7

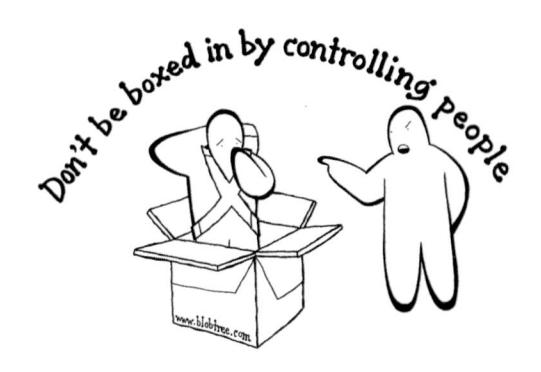

Don't be boxed in by controlling people

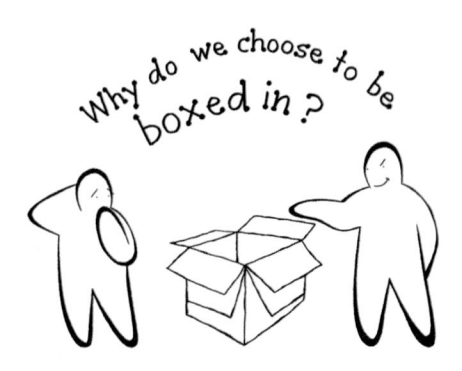

Why do we choose to be boxed in?

My family life was a mix of safety and adventure!

www.blobtree.com

Could we imagine leaving our safe space?

www.blobtree.com

Controlling people often work in groups

www.blobtree.com

Choice masks the feeling of control

We can be controlled in a variety of ways

www.blobtree.com

It's easier to see the needs of others + miss our own

www.blobtree.com

Our feelings like to be our CEO and control us

www.blobtree.com

Safety is not the same as control

www.blobtree.com

www.blobtree.com

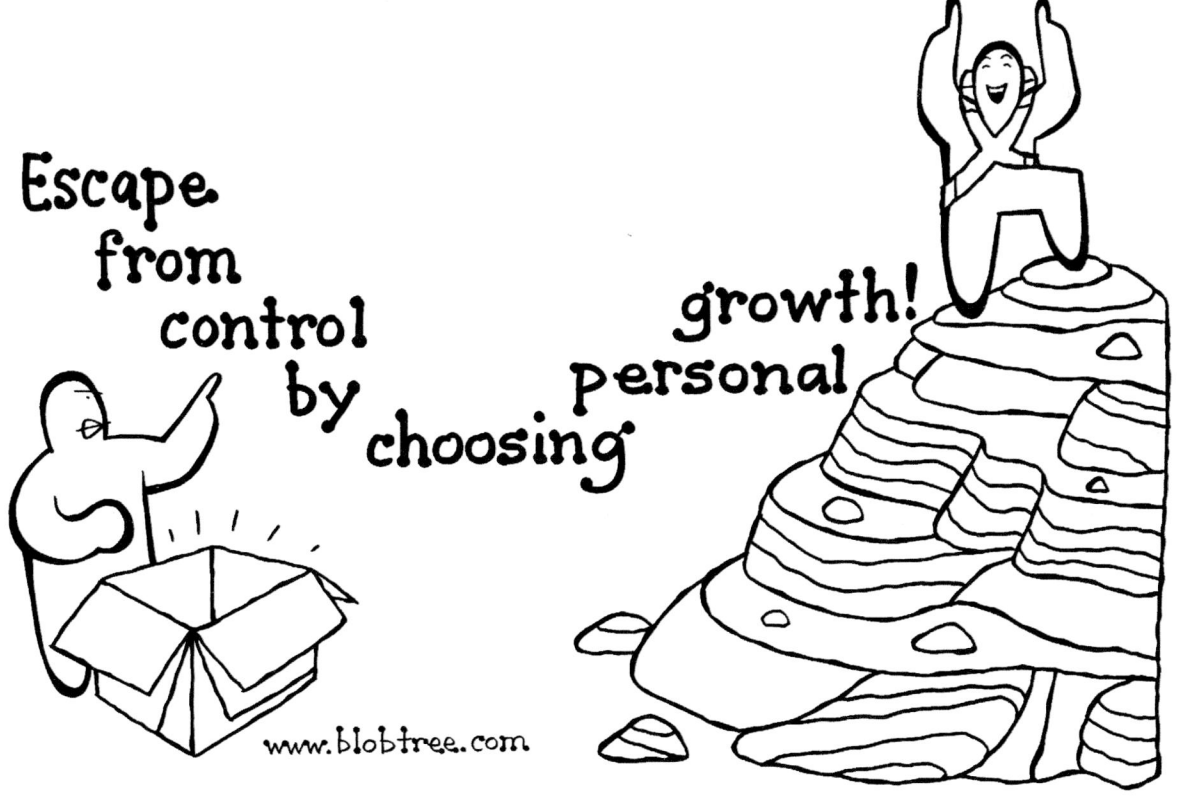

Escape from control by choosing personal growth!

www.blobtree.com

Some wish to control the whole world!

www.blobtree.com

All my life I longed for my own

safe space

www.blobtree.com

Fear may cause us to seek safety at any price

www.blobtree.com

Eventually, people resist being controlled

www.blobtree.com

www.blobtree.com